HOMOSEXUALITY

Good Choice Or Bad Choice?

David P. Therrien

"Scripture quotations taken from the New American Standard Bible®,
Copyright © 1960, 1962, 1963, 1968, 1971, 1972, 1973,
1975, 1977, 1995 by The Lockman Foundation
Used by permission." (www.Lockman.org)

ISBN: 1514817462
ISBN-13: 9781514817469

DEDICATION

This book is dedicated to two groups of people.
It is dedicated to those who have been swept up in the popular, cultural opinion in the hope that you may find and embrace Truth.
It is also dedicated to the people who are not afraid to go against the flow of popular, cultural opinion.

CONTENTS

DAVID P. THERRIEN

ACKNOWLEDGEMENTS

Thank you David Sherry who was so faithful in assuring this book was of the highest literary quality. Your efforts are greatly appreciated.

DAVID P. THERRIEN

WHY I WROTE THIS BOOK

We are living in a time of changing culture, and with these changes, people have found themselves on both sides of the homosexual conversation. There are those who believe in the homosexual way of life so much, that they have given their lives to it. On the other side, there are those who are so adamantly against it, that they either have become hostile and intolerant in their response or there are those who are labeled hostile and intolerant who disagree. And there are those in the middle who are indifferent to the whole thing. To them it is a do as you please mentality, just as long as you don't hurt anybody.

By writing this book, I am trying to bring the conversation to a place where the discussion is respectful and dignified. At the end, people will make their own decisions as to the veracity of living in a same sex relationship.

So let's have a conversation and honestly and objectively examine this matter, perhaps not so much in the light of today, but in the light of eternity.

INTRODUCTION

The book you are about to read was not an easy one to write. Anything of a sensitive nature always stands the chance of hurting someone in their innermost being. This is certainly not the intention of the author.

The subject of homosexuality has come front and center in the American culture and it has also become a political force. But is life all about politics? Hopefully, after reading this book, the reader will see that it is not.

To gain the best insight into this topic,

the reader must delve into these pages with honesty and openness. One can never learn when they take their own preconceived notions into the classroom.

I, the author, also believe that "all" people are made in the image of God, and therefore, there is a tremendous value ascribed to each one. Whatever side of the aisle you may find yourself on, know that you are loved, valued and of the utmost importance to your Creator. He gave you the opportunity for life so you can walk with Him and He can, when needed, carry you.

May the reading of this book give you a freedom that you have never truly known before.

Chapter 1

Everyone Needs Love

Who doesn't need to be loved and give love? We are made for that very reason. Love is a two-edged sword. It is that which gives the greatest satisfaction and fulfillment, and it is that which inflicts the greatest hurt. How can one and the same thing have two different outcomes?

It can bring about two different outcomes because the nature of mankind is flawed. We are born with original sin and that has distorted our view of love and just about everything else in life. We steal and lie, then justify it. It is inbred in us from birth. A little child steals a cookie from the cookie jar before dinner and then lies about it. Where did that come from? It wasn't a learned behavior, it is an inbred behavior. Of all the things that suffer in life from this inbred sinful nature, love suffers the most.

When we seek love, we often view it as receiving more than giving. Yet, true love is an act of giving. We have made love selfish.

There is a song from the 70's that says; "I'm looking for love in all the wrong places, looking for love in too many faces..." Why does this happen? Because we need love.

Sometimes people fail at love and they vow they will never love again. Others have been so hurt in love that they would rather receive love from someone of the same sex, hoping never to experience the pain of broken love again. But one thing cannot be denied, we all need love.

Love is not to be confused with sex. Sex is a temporal, physical activity that can bring satisfaction to one or two people engaging in it. But it is temporal, physical and it does wax old.

But love is enduring. Love lives long after the sexual desires have died. Love is more complete, therefore, more fulfilling. It lives on through the day and the night. It survives the storms of life and is always putting the other person first. That's what love does. You know you are loving when you put the other person ahead of yourself.

So you see, love doesn't have to be sexual. That is only a brief intermission in the daily routine of living. But the life is benefitted when love rules from sun up to sun down.

Chapter 2

Understanding Homosexuality

Both the church and modern culture are divided in their understanding of what homosexuality is and how homosexual people should be treated. And when a subject generates such an emotional response as homosexuality does, many people are tempted to avoid it all together. But God has given us His Word which addresses all the issues of life so no issue at all need ever be avoided.

Think of the Bible as God's rule for life,

for that is what it is. It is a gift from the Creator of life. The Bible is called the "Canon of Scripture." Canon means "rule". It is the rule of life, the roadmap for the journey. If the Bible is not your roadmap, then what is? What map are you following for your own personal journey? Once this is settled in your heart, you will find His wisdom very inviting.

Let's begin to answer some questions. The first question is, "What is homosexuality?"

Homosexuality refers to two things: a condition and a behavior.

The Homosexual Condition vs. Behavior

Homosexuality is commonly referred to as an orientation. This is where a person is sexually attracted to a member or members of the same sex. The inward attraction is a "condition." But homosexual "behavior" is different. Homosexual behavior is any form of sexual activity between two members of the same sex. One is an attraction and one is a behavior. Let us note that an attraction does not give license to a behavior.

If someone was attracted to a beautiful diamond ring in the window of a jewelry store, that doesn't justify the behavior to steal the ring. There is a difference between homosexual attraction and homosexual behavior.

People do not generally choose the homosexual condition. There are many tendencies ingrained in people that show themselves early in life. You could say that the condition is inborn but the behavior is a matter of choice. Choice is what we do with our desires. Everyone has desires. Some of those desires are good and some are not so good. But we are responsible, not for the desires but for how we act on those desires. We all have inborn inclinations, and the secret to life is to bring those inclinations under control. That's called "self-control." The evidence of this is in the fact that there is good and evil in the world. We all have an inbred inclination to evil.

What Causes Homosexuality?

Practicing homosexuals believe that their sexuality is inherited and therefore, not a behavior but a condition. It is involuntary and should be considered morally neutral.

If a homosexual tendency was genetically inborn, the question remains, is the inborn tendency beyond one's control? Are all the tendencies we have beyond our ability to control them? There are tendencies to overeat, overspend and over talk.

What do we do with the men who have an inborn tendency to lust after women or women after men? What would that do to the marriage contract of fidelity if people were allowed to act on those tendencies while married? What do we do with people who have a sexual lust for children? There are also those who have inherited a lust for alcohol either through genetics or learned behavior.

We would find that promiscuity, pedophilia and alcoholism would result from unchecked inner lusts.

As real as these tendencies are, they would not be considered socially acceptable. Those who engage in these practices are usually referred to counselling and in some cases, jail time.

Being genetically inclined to do immoral things does not make immoral behavior right. The law does not ignore evil doers because of their flawed, sinful nature. Rather, the law comes down on people for the choices they made regarding their sinful nature.

Single individuals have a desire for fulfillment from the opposite sex. But they are still called to a life of purity. Though there are those who would disagree with this, the evidence supports a life of abstinence when not married is a much safer and healthier life.

The one who commits adultery with a woman is lacking sense; he who would destroy himself does it.

Proverbs 6:32

Let's think for a moment about those that suffer from the tendency of road rage. These are people that are easily upset by other drivers. Their tendency would be to somehow, someway take revenge on the driver who upset them. We can all agree that people who suffer from road rage are a hazard to other drivers and even themselves.

Just because you feel like doing something, is no reason to do it. This world would be even crazier than it is if everyone did what they felt like doing with no self-control at all. We know that we have to restrain ourselves and bring our particular tendencies under control.

Psychologists give us several reasons for homosexual tendencies. One reason is a faulty relationship with a parent of the same sex. Another cause, they say, is a weak or absent father. He may be absent physically or absent emotionally, failing to give the support his child needs in the formative years.

A domineering mother and the lack of bonding with peers, they say, also contribute to homosexual tendencies. Sexual abuse in some cases and even the influence of other homosexuals can be factors in someone being brought into the culture of homosexuality.

Another factor is the promoting of the homosexual lifestyle in our fields of entertainment and even more directly, in the institutions of learning, our schools.

The need that led to this condition is likely, legitimate. No one can argue the fact that someone can have an inborn tendency, or perhaps a domineering mother or an absent father, or the fact that they've been abused, or they never made friends with their peers. Those are legitimate causes, but the fulfillment of that need is in question.

Inherited Genetic Tendencies

It has been established that inherited characteristics that are not passed down to the next generation are eliminated from the gene pool. As homosexuals do not reproduce as heterosexuals are able to do, their numbers would diminish over time. With every generation there would be less and less homosexual tendencies.

Today, there is no indication of a decline in homosexual activity.

A final cause for the popularity of homosexuality is experimentation. Many young people are being encouraged to "experiment" with this new way of love. It's another sexual revolution, only taken to the next level. With the approval of the adult world, especially those who are looked up to by our young people, curiosity and experimentation are adding to the spread of this lifestyle, making it socially acceptable.

Chapter 3

The Bible Is Our Manual For Life

This chapter is important because everyone has their own opinion regarding the issues of life. Yet, life cannot perpetuate itself at the highest level without a standard to live by. Anything less would be chaos that leads to destruction. There are cultures all over the world that lack high standards with the result that women have no rights, they are abused, children are made slaves and violence is considered a normal way of life.

Think of the instructions we need to get

along in life. We need to learn a manual to drive a car, and we all have to read the same manual. You need a manual (cookbook) to make that particular meal. A manual is needed to assemble that TV stand. Doctors refer to their medical manuals to treat their patients. So how can we not have a manual to help us to live a healthy and wholesome life?

What would life be like if we all made up our own way of driving our cars? Someone has a Hummer or Land Rover. They're made for going over rough terrain, like your front yard. I guess if everyone makes up their own driving rules, then we have to let them drive over our front yards!

Someone else says, I don't have to own my own car. I can use any car I want to. I'll just hot wire it. We would have to say, well, if that's how you feel and that's your standard, I guess so.

No, we don't let people make up their

own rules when it comes to driving automobiles but when it comes to life, we let people make up their own rules.

God's manual for life is the rule of life. It is the instruction book for true fulfillment. And it takes great humility to put oneself under the authority of that book. Humility says I will put myself under the authority of God's book and I will let it dictate to me how I am going to live my life. The prideful always do it their own way, and the result is usually regret.

In His love, God has given us instructions to insure a healthy life on earth and access into heaven when life is finished here. The Bible is not a hate book but a love letter. Listen to the Apostle Paul's letter to Timothy;

But we know that the Law is good if one uses it lawfully, realizing the fact that law is not made for a righteous person, but for those who are lawless and rebellious, for the ungodly and sinners, for the unholy and profane, for those who will kill their fathers or mothers, for murderers and immoral men and homosexuals and kidnappers and liars and perjurers, and whatever else is contrary to sound teaching, according to the glorious gospel of the blessed God, with which I have been entrusted.

Timothy 1:8-11

Paul sees his life as God's messenger to bring God's message of hope to a lost and dying world. And many of those who are lost and dying do not even realize it.

Chapter 4

The Justice Of God

God is infinitely just and He would never judge a behavior where people have no responsibility for engaging in it.

Yet, God is very clear with regard to His thoughts on homosexuality.

Do you not know that the unrighteous shall not inherit the kingdom of God? Do not be deceived, neither fornicators, nor idolaters, nor adulterers, nor effeminate, nor homosexuals, nor thieves, nor the covetous, nor drunkards, nor revilers, nor

swindlers, shall inherit the kingdom of God.
I Corinthians 6:9

The Apostle Paul, in this letter to the Corinthians is talking about lifestyle. The lifestyle of these behaviors mentioned above is a sign that this person is not born of God, therefore, alienated from God and His kingdom.

God is saying in His Word, that when any of these lifestyles depict you, you will not get into the kingdom of God. This is the lifestyle of the unregenerate person. The unregenerate person has not yet found the new life in Christ that He provides through His sacrifice on the cross and one's faith in that work.

When Paul wrote, *nor effeminate... shall inherit the kingdom of God...* he was talking about a young boy who was kept by a practicing homosexual adult for sexual pleasure. This was very common in the ancient world among the Romans and Greeks.

This warning to the Christians in Corinth is given against the background of incest, homosexuality, pedophilia and other unnatural sexual vices which were commonly practiced in his day.

Because this culture was socially accepted, the church had to be warned against allowing or falling into this behavior. Socrates said fourteen of the first fifteen Roman Emperors practiced homosexuality.

The reason God prohibits certain behaviors is because He has something better in mind. Here, Paul was given the mission to inform the people of Corinth, Greece of that.

This is not a singling out of homosexuality. As mentioned above, any lifestyle of sin robs the individual of all that God has for them. Stealing, lying, coveting, brawlers and dishonest people all give evidence of still abiding in the fallen nature without the regenerating power of the Holy Spirit in their life.

Temptation vs. Practice

The condemnation is not in being tempted in these areas. All people are subject to temptation. Jesus was subject to temptation.

We have a High Priest Who has been tempted in all things, as we are, yet without sin.

Hebrews 4:15

Because Jesus was tempted in the human realm, He can identify with our temptations and come to our aid when we are tempted.

For since He, Himself was tempted in that which He has suffered, He is able to

come to the aid of those who are tempted.
Hebrews 2:18

The condemnation is in the practice of those things.

We are not judged because of our tendencies, inclinations or desires. Our battle in life is to try to bring those things under control. But when we take the next step and act on those temptations God brings in the judgment.

Chapter 5

When You Turn Your Back On God

In His love, God has provided all that we need for a healthy and fulfilling life. He is the Creator and knows what works best. But there are consequences when we turn from those dictates and go another way.

The reason any nation, society, family or individual falls into a lifestyle of dissatisfaction, unfulfillment and, in some cases, even destruction is because they have turned their face from God.

When we turn our face from God there is only one other alternative, we turn our face upon ourselves. We then put ourselves in a place where God belongs. Rather than God being on the throne of our life and directing our steps through justice, love and mercy, we direct our own steps. The motivation to do this is our flesh; our own sinful nature. The first step is discontentment, then discouragement, which then leads to acts of destruction. Greed, jealousy, selfishness, control and criticism become our guide. When we follow those steps long enough they begin to look like normal behaviors.

The Bible outlines what is called, "the works of the flesh." We must be careful that they not become the norm for our lives.

Now the deeds of the flesh are evident, which are: immorality, impurity, sensuality,

idolatry, sorcery, enmities, strife, jealousy,
outbursts of anger, disputes,
dissensions, factions,
envying, drunkenness, carousing, and
things like these, of which I forewarn
you, just as I have forewarned you, that
those who practice such things will not
inherit the kingdom of God.
Galatians 5:19-21

That is why it is so important not to turn your face away from God in any struggle or situation. When you turn your face from God you are at the beginning of the end.

In contrast, let us note the "fruit of the Spirit" in a believer's life.

But the fruit of the Spirit is love, joy, peace,
patience, kindness, goodness,
faithfulness,
gentleness, self-control; against such things
there is no law.

Galatians 5:22-23

The difference is obvious. Which would you rather have describe your life?

It is very dangerous not to consider God or His Word. When you don't consider God, you can only consider yourself.

The Three-fold War

1. Self

At this juncture, one finds himself/herself in a battle on three fronts. The first battle is against the self. This is because there is a deviation from the person who you are, naturally. This deviation creates an identity crisis. Who am I? Who should I be? What should I do? These questions begin to stir in the soul and without self-control, can reap havoc in one's mind. Self-doubt also begins to creep in and with the flow of society you are swept in the wrong direction and it only intensifies the battle.

2. Society

Society is not constructed for like-gender sexual relationships. The family framework requires a male, father figure and a female, mother figure. Both bring something different to the table which growing children need. That is why even single parent families are strained. A mother has to play two roles or likewise in other situations, a father has to play a dual role. Though these single parents do the best they can and do have a degree of success, they would agree that a combination of mother and father would do better. It has been that way since the beginning and we even see it in the animal kingdom.

3. Perpetuation Of The Human Race

This battle is against the human race, itself. For mankind to perpetuate itself, there must be egg and seed. A homosexual couple cannot produce what is required to perpetuate the human race. It is biologically impossible. Therefore, we can draw the conclusion that if homosexuality were the norm for every human being, mankind would die out in one generation. But if heterosexuality were the norm for every human being, mankind would continue as it always has.

Consider these three fronts where the battle is being waged. A general cannot wage war based on his emotions, he must use the facts before him. How he feels will not help him on the battle field. The tactics he has learned and the discipline of his training will result in his success.

So it is as we consider the battlefront

of homosexuality. It is a very emotional topic but emotions will not win the battle, only the facts and self-discipline of the mind.

Chapter 6

A Lust-driven King

Lust is a powerful force. It is inbred in all people. It is a controlling factor, an appetite that must be subdued. The following is a true story of a man who either could not or would not subdue his lustful appetite. We will trace the steps of his downfall.

"Then it happened in the spring, at the time when kings go out to battle...but this king stayed at home." (I Samuel 11)

The first thing we discover is that the king was in the wrong place at the wrong time. He should have been at his kingly duty, leading his men in battle. Every man and woman should find themselves doing what they should be doing. To lag behind in one's responsibilities, is to set yourself up for trouble.

The king was napping on the flat roof of his house when he got up from his bed, went over to his terrace, looked down and saw a woman bathing. She was a beautiful woman and the lust in his heart began to stir.

Rather than check himself, he entertained the situation and took the next step. He inquired from his servant who this beautiful woman might be.

When lust begins to dictate to the heart it is like putting a kayak into the beginning of a rushing river. The beginning of the river seems very calm and you have no idea of the dangerous rapids that are waiting. Soon the kayak is caught up in the flow.

It was told to the king who she was and who her husband was. That should have been the end of it. She was married. And she was married to one of the king's most valiant soldiers who was on the battlefield.

As the waters began to rush, he sent for her anyway and she lay with him. Her cooperation with the king may make you wonder as to her being an accomplice in this matter but remember, he was the king!

Not long after, she informed the king she was with his child. The king had an idea that he thought would surely cover his dilemma. You see, lust never stops thinking. He sent for her husband to return from the battlefield to spend some time with his wife. He did return from the field but, being the valiant soldier that he was, he refused to go home to find pleasure when his men were still in the trenches.

But lust is very resourceful. When the king discovered this, he prepared a meal with him and got him drunk. He thought, surely he will go home to his wife now. But again, he slept in the doorway of the king's house.

Once in the rapids, there is no turning back. Lust can take such a hold on a person that they become a prisoner to that lust and can only go deeper into horrific behavior.

The king wrote a note, sent it back with the soldier with instructions to give it to his commander. The note instructed the commander to put the soldier on the front line in the fiercest part of the battle where he would be killed. The obedient commander did as he was instructed and the soldier was killed. Shortly after, the king took his widow as his own wife.

A short time later, a prophet came to the king to report an incident. He told the king there were two men in a city, a rich man and a poor man. The rich man had many flocks and herds. The poor man had nothing but one little ewe lamb. It grew up together with him and his children. It would eat of his bread and drink of his cup and lie in his bosom. The lamb was like a daughter to him.

Now a traveler came to the rich man and he was unwilling to take from his own flock or his own herd to prepare food for the traveler. Rather, he took the poor man's ewe lamb and prepared it for the man who had come to him.

Then the king's anger burned greatly against the man and he said to the prophet, "As the Lord lives, surely the man who has done this deserves to die." He must make restitution for the lamb fourfold because he did this and had no compassion." The prophet said to the king, "You are the man! You have struck down your soldier and have taken his wife to be your wife. Now, trouble will never depart from your house."

The king's life was never the same again. There was always conflict in his family and within a year, the baby born to him died.

Can you see the power of the rushing river of lust? Once in the white water, it is very difficult, if not impossible to get out. This is why lust has to be checked in the beginning stages. Whether it is lust for money, power, control, recognition, a member of the opposite sex or the same sex, it must be brought under control. It is a condition that must not be allowed to turn into a behavior.

Chapter 7

On The Street Interviews

We hit the streets and asked people what was their take on homosexuality.

Here is what we found.

Question:

"What do think about Homosexuality?"

A young man said; "It's hard to accept, it makes a lot of people feel uncomfortable."

A young girl said; "Me personally? No, I don't have a problem with it. Morally, I don't think there is anything wrong with it. I have people in my family who have different opinions about it so I have no problem with it."

An older woman said; "I'm going to be honest with you. I feel whatever today makes you happy, you do it. If it's two girls, two guys, go right ahead. If it's going to make you happy."

Another young girl said, "If you're not attracted to the opposite sex, then, whatever."

Another young man said, "I think that people should be able to live their lives as they wish as long as they are not harming another person."

Next question:
"Is homosexuality a healthy lifestyle?"

A young girl answered; "I don't see anything wrong with it. It's probably as healthy as a regular relationship."

Another young girl responded; "I think it's probably more healthier because if you are going out with someone the same sex as you, you understand them more because they're the same as you."

Another young girl said; "I guess it's healthier if you're happy."

An older woman responded; "Not really. I don't believe it's healthy but that's not my choice, it's their choice that they're going to have to live with."

Another young girl said; "Sure, I have a lot of gay friends and I don't see that there's anything unhealthy about it."

A young man said; "No less healthy than heterosexuality."

Another young man said; "It would be the same if you were a heterosexual and played the field. You're going to run into the same communicable diseases. Sexual morality or immorality is the same thing whether you are a homosexual or a heterosexual."

Final question:
"How do you think God views the homosexual lifestyle?"

A young girl said; "God should love everybody and accept them no matter what and I don't think you can help being homosexual because there is evidence now that it is a genetic thing."

A young man said; "I don't think God worries too much about that. He has more important issues."

A young girl said; "I don't actually believe in Jesus."

Another young girl said; "I'm not really religious but I think God would accept you for who you are, however you are."

A young man said; "God doesn't go for it at all. One of the worst things of the Christian church is to have someone among their ranks to say it's okay."

Take a moment and think about those answers. Are they the product of deep thought and soul-searching? Are they the product of popular, cultural opinion? Are they merely one's own desire of what they want it to be? This is why truth is so important: it puts everybody on the same page.

My Remarks Regarding The On The Street Interview

The people voiced their own opinions about homosexuality, but I struggle with where they get their information.

It is interesting how people tell God how and what He is to be. If you go back to the first response to the final question which was, "How do you think God views the homosexual lifestyle?" she responded, "God should love everybody and accept them no matter what." That is the part of the problem today; when people determine what God should be like. I don't think you would want that done to you, would you Dear Reader?

The truth is that God does love every one of the interviewees said. Whether they believe in Jesus or not, homosexual or heterosexual, He died and shed His blood for every one of them. They all have the option to believe in Him and acknowledge Him as the Savior that He is. When they do, regeneration takes place and the heart is made new.

Without the wisdom of God we are left with the wisdom of man. When people say they should be able to do anything that makes them happy, that opens up a whole new set of rules, or should I say "non-rules."

That reasoning doesn't make sense when it comes to the practical way of life. Doing whatever I want to make me happy doesn't work when grocery shopping, driving my car, at work or playing sports. There are always rules and guides to follow.

I have to pay what the grocery store says I must pay for my groceries. I cannot set my own prices.

If your son strikes out playing little league, you can't pick him up and run to first base. That is not in the rule book. And what would the game look like if every parent did that?

The reasoning for finding happiness is flawed. This is why we need to be faithful to God and His Word. In there, we have honest, sensible reasoning. That's what keeps us all playing by the same rules. When we all play by the same rules, the game is more enjoyable. The outcome is more fair and the diligent are rewarded.

Chapter 8
Arguments For And Against Homosexuality

For

Many people, homosexual and not, justify the behavior for various reasons. They would say everyone has the right to live as they choose. That is true, as long as they do not break the law or hurt others. It is also argued that consenting adults should be able to do as they please and are not answerable to anyone. Again, that is agreed. For many, if not all people, are on a pursuit of happiness so their mantra is, "Whatever makes you happy, do it."

Many homosexuals have also chosen to be in a monogamous relationship because of love. It is agreed once again that people who love each other have the right to be in a monogamous relationship.

Against

There are three simple reasons that disqualify homosexuality as a legitimate lifestyle:

1. It was not that way in the beginning.

God created man in His own image, in the image of God He created him, male and female, he created them.

Genesis 1:27

Here, mankind is represented by a male and female union.

After creating Adam, God formed Eve and brought her to him to complete him.

The LORD God fashioned into a woman the rib which He had taken from the man, and brought her to the man.
The man said, "This is now bone of my bones, and flesh of my flesh; she shall be called Woman, because she was taken out of Man."
For this reason a man shall leave his father and his mother, and be joined to his wife; and they shall become one flesh.
Genesis 2:22-24

2. It cannot produce offspring to perpetuate the human race.

God blessed them; and God said to them, "Be fruitful and multiply, and fill the earth, and subdue it; and rule over the fish of the sea and over the birds of the sky and over every living thing that moves on the earth."
Genesis 1:28

3. It is unnatural; against nature.

This principle below did not disappear from current day mandates.

For even though they knew God, they did not honor Him as God or give thanks, but they became futile in their speculations and their foolish heart was darkened. Romans 1:21

For this reason God gave them over to degrading passions; for their women exchanged the natural function for that which is unnatural,

and in the same way also the men abandoned the natural function of the woman and burned in their desire toward one another, men with men committing indecent acts and receiving in their own persons the due penalty of their error.

And just as they did not see fit to

acknowledge God any longer, God gave them over to a depraved mind, to do those things which are not proper, Romans 1:26-28

although they know the ordinance of God, that those who practice such things are worthy of death, they not only do the same, but also give hearty approval to those who practice them. Romans 1:32

Their outrageous conduct was not due to total ignorance of what God required, but to self-will and rebellion.

When they *give hearty approval* (v.32), they are applauding, rather than regretting, the sins of others.

Divine Judgment on homosexuality:

Homosexuality is judged like many other sins.

Or do you not know that the unrighteous will not inherit the kingdom of God? Do not be deceived; neither fornicators, nor idolaters, nor adulterers, nor effeminate, nor homosexuals,

nor thieves, nor the covetous, nor drunkards, nor revilers, nor swindlers, will inherit the kingdom of God.
I Corinthians 6:9-10

We are all born sinners. Some have a bent toward a particular sin. Having a temptation toward any particular sin is not sin, but it also does not give one the right to engage in that sin. That is how it becomes sin.

- lying
- murder
- temper tantrums
- sexual drive

Yet, any person that is caught up in a sin can change.

Such <u>were</u> some of you; but you were

washed, but you were sanctified, but you were justified in the name of the Lord Jesus Christ and in the Spirit of our God.

I Corinthians 6:11

The problem with sin today is that many people do not want to change. It is easier to say it is not a sin than to call it sin and turn from it. But it "can" be done.

There is hope for all sinners in Jesus Christ. We all stand on equal ground at the foot of the cross.

Chapter 9
God's Answer To Homosexuality

Because God is the Author life and He knows what works best for us and because He loves us, He has an answer for Homosexuality.

For this reason God gave them over to degrading passions; for their women exchanged the natural function for that which is unnatural, and in the same way also the men abandoned the natural function of the woman and burned in their desire toward one another, men with men committing indecent acts and receiving in their own persons the due penalty of their error.

And just as they did not see fit to acknowledge God any longer, God gave them over to a depraved mind, to do those things which are not proper.

Romans 1:26-28

A Sad Result

When someone fails to acknowledge God, He turns them over to a depraved mind. Then abnormal becomes normal and normal becomes abnormal.

If there is something that you want so badly, sometimes God will give it; whether good or bad, right or wrong, because it is about choice. We choose what we want in life because God gave us the gift of free will.

Moses spoke for God when he said to the people of Israel:

> *See, I have set before you today life and prosperity, death and adversity; in that I command you today to love the Lord your God, to walk in His ways, to keep His commandments and His statutes, and His judgments, that you may live and multiply, and that the Lord your God may bless you in the land..."*
>
> Deuteronomy 30:15-16

Here, God says to choose, but to choose life – so you and your descendants will have life. God gives the choice but He also gives the answer.

On the contrary, to fail in this area is to be turned over to a depraved mind. And a depraved mind results in a lifestyle that will never lead to real fulfillment and a relationship with God. And more dangerously, a depraved mind never recognizes its depravity.

Chapter 10

A Christian's Attitude Toward Homosexuals

Christians have a spiritual mandate to love and care for all people all over the world. People are made in the image of God and therefore, are entitled to be treated with respect and dignity; even those who are living in immoral circumstances.

Christians have a particular standard that they are to live by. There is no place for hatred, hurtful jokes, degrading remarks or other forms of rejection toward those that are homosexual. They should be treated like anyone else.

We cannot hope to win others to Christ if we insult them, wound them, hurt them, mock them or make fun of them. We also apply this truth to a person's religious belief. You never make degrading remarks about another person's religion. We should never make degrading remarks – period!

Winning someone to Christ begins with accepting them right where they are, as God has done for us. And the girl in the interview was right: God does love all people, and He does accept us. But, He cannot accept us into a holy heaven if we are void of the Holy Spirit. It takes being indwelt by the Holy Spirit to live in heaven and in the presence of God. The love others see in God's people should lead them to the God who created them and loves them too.

Chapter 11

Jesus, Friend Of Sinners

Jesus, Himself was a friend of sinners and He hated the hypocrisy of the religious, judgmental leaders of His day; especially those who lacked love for other people.

The scribes and the Pharisees have seated themselves in the chair of Moses; therefore all that they tell you, do and observe, but do not do according to their deeds; for they say things and do not do them.

They tie up heavy burdens and lay them on men's shoulders, but they themselves are unwilling to move them with so much as a finger.
Mathew 23:2-4

Jesus was condemned by the religious crowd for hanging out with sinners; the tax collectors and prostitutes. The reason He did was because He said "He came for those who need a physician." Jesus always found an audience with those who knew they needed to change – and they wanted to change. In their honesty, they knew there was a better way and they believed Jesus could provide that.

Jesus not only loves all people but He calls us to love all people. We are called to love Christians, non-Christians, drug addicts, gamblers, homosexuals, thieves and people in general. Now, that doesn't mean we come alongside them and encourage them in those behaviors, but it does mean that we love them, treat them with dignity and respect with the hope of giving them the truth of the Gospel, that they would be set free. We show them love and acceptance so they would find hope in Jesus Christ. That's the role of the believer in Christ.

Of all in the people in the world, it should be the Christian that others can come to in their time of need. They would be accepted and loved but also given truth. They will not be condemned for their decisions and lifestyle they are living.

Chapter 12

What Do I Do If I Am A Homosexual?

If you believe that you are homosexual and you have a heart after God, there is something you can do. Like any other heterosexual that is not married, refrain from sexual behavior. Remember, it is a desire, a strong desire but a desire that needs to be brought under control. People have all kinds of tendencies that must be brought under control. The tendency to over spend, over eat, over drink, to take recreational drugs, if not checked, can and will destroy a life.

God is faithful, He is for you and not against you. Jesus, Himself understood temptation in His human form but He never gave in to it. Temptation is a reality in this world, and constant battle that we fight, but God gives us the strength to make the right decisions in time of need.

Once you decide to refrain from sexual, immoral behavior, get into the Word of God.

The Psalmist wrote;

Thy Word is a lamp to my feet and a
light to my path.

Ps 119:105

Let God's Word direct your steps. That's humility; putting yourself under the Word of God.

Finally, live the rest of your life for God and His desires for your life. Find out what God wants you to do with your life and pursue that course. This is not always the easiest thing to do, though it is the right thing.

Paul said to the Christians in Rome;

I urge you therefore, brethren, by the mercies of God, to present your bodies a living and holy sacrifice, acceptable to God, which is your spiritual (reasonable) service of worship.

Romans 12:1

Sacrifice means that we have areas in our life that we have to die to. We need to give them over to God. We cannot live a life pleasing to God while carrying those things we have to crucify. God expects this of all people, to crucify those areas that are a hindrance to their spiritual growth and their personal relationship with Him.

In the next verse, Paul said;

And do not be conformed to this world.

Romans 12:2

If you remember the interviews you read about previously, you read opinions that have been formed according to this world. They reflect the philosophy of this world system and not of God. As a matter of fact, they are contradictory in all facets of life and becoming more so with each generation.

So the question becomes, which philosophy will I choose to live by? If you choose to live according to this world's system, then let everyone do as they please and make up their own rules. Humankind is not wise enough to make up their own rules. The result is always chaos and destruction. And don't forget, you are also giving people the right to infringe on your life too.

Have you noticed that the system of the world is tolerant to everything except God and Christianity? That violates its own standard of independence and letting people choose for themselves.

I can refrain from conforming to the system of the world by renewing my mind in the Word of God. Yes, it is a washing of the brain, the mind and the thoughts. As I cultivate clean thoughts, God's thoughts, I cultivate a purposeful and fulfilling life.

Paul's final thought is;

So that you may prove what the will of God is, that which is good, and acceptable and perfect.

Romans 12:2

God's will for every person is good, acceptable and perfect. By living in the will of God through being a living sacrifice, your life will be divinely good, acceptable to Him and perfect, which means complete.

Chapter 13

It's Interesting

Back in chapter 8 we noted a passage of Scripture that outlined several practices that God seeks to deliver people from. In that list, society seems to agree with God, except for one of them. Here they are again.

Or do you not know that the unrighteous will not inherit the kingdom of God? Do not be deceived; neither fornicators, nor idolaters, nor adulterers, nor effeminate, nor homosexuals, nor thieves, nor the

covetous, nor drunkards, nor revilers,
nor swindlers, will inherit the kingdom
of God.

I Corinthians 6:9-10

Let's take a look at these.

"Fornication" is sexual activity outside of marriage, but I don't think any caring parent would want their daughter sleeping around. People who worship things, "idolaters", look weird to others who do such things. "Adultery" is frowned upon by the masses. Though it happens, it is not considered a noble deed.

There are no trophies given out to those who "steal" from others. Society actually puts those people in jail. Those who "covet" and then act on it become thieves and end up in jail or at the least, live in jealousy.

We see driving accidents on the news all the time caused by intoxicated people.

The organization, "Mothers Against Drunk Drivers" does their best to keep them off the roads. How much hurt and pain has been caused by "drunken" people? Sometimes, they turn into "revilers." These people are always looking for a fight. And the "swindlers?" Well, corporate greed and corrupt politicians who tread this path find their reputations easily ruined. This behavior also fractures a society and its economy.

Now the interesting part. Homosexuality is the only practice mentioned in that group that is applauded by our society. That seems strange to me. How about you? Why are all the other practices looked down upon, even punished, but not homosexuality? It is not only not looked down upon it is actually celebrated. It is seen as a good thing and as a mark of progress. In some circles, it is even compared to the freeing of the slaves in early Americana.

The Moral Compass

The Scriptures above give evidence that we have a moral compass within us. It shows us which way to go to preserve the self-life and society. When we follow the direction of the compass, we find ourselves heading in the direction we should be going. But to ignore the compass is to risk becoming lost or sailing into the rocks.

We are beginning to move away from the use of the moral compass, and like the great nations of ancient Greece and Rome, we are being directed by lust.

Lust is an unholy desire. It comes in many forms. There is lust for power, lust for money, lust for control and lust for sex. When any of these lusts guide one's life, it will always result in disaster. And when the people of a society succumb to these lusts, like Greece and Rome, it results in their downfall. It begins the corrosion from the inside.

This would be a good time to lead into Shelley's Story. It is the testimony of a former, practicing lesbian, who was in the culture for nine years. Listen as she traces her story from just a little girl of eight years old, into her twenty's and where she is today.

Chapter 14

Shelley's Story

My name is Shelley and I would like to share my story with you. I began feeling a lustful stirring in me when I was in high school. Sometimes when I would hug a friend I would feel a strong, sexual feeling. I began to wonder about myself.

But it really didn't begin there. When I was only eight years old a man exposed himself to me and that shock triggered something inside of me. It became a dislike for men. At twenty-one years old

I began drinking and was with a man. That turned into a date rape and that turned me off to men completely. I began to back away from any heterosexual relationship just for the sake of protection. I was terrified of all men.

My mom and dad were not affectionate people. I never had the nurturing or caresses that a young person needs to feel secure in herself. Experiences in my earlier life made me trust men less and I found an attraction to women.

In my mid-twenties I entered a convent. At times I felt a strong connection to God. I grew up in the Roman Catholic religion and I was taught that a relationship with God as strongly as I felt, must mean I am called by God to the religious life.

A year later, while in the convent, I met a woman outside of the convent and experimented with homosexuality and eventually, I left the convent. I grew up a Roman Catholic and had a belief in Jesus Christ. Godly convictions set in frequently and warned me not to fall into this lifestyle. But like so many other women who were lured into homosexuality, the pull of sex and lust due to alcohol was no match for my convictions. In that relationship I felt loved and accepted. My partner, Kathy, also had a child, a young daughter of four years old that really drew me in. This looked and felt so right. I remained in that monogamous relationship for nine years.

During that time, I felt God's pull to get out. That was Divine timing because I was invited to attend a Bill Gothard seminar. During the seminar he told everyone not to miss the last day. I took that day off from work and attended. It was made for me. He showed me clearly in the Bible that homosexuality was not of God. He used the Word to back up his teaching. That night I remember thinking, I can't even tell my earthly father about this relationship, how can I face my heavenly Father someday regarding this lifestyle? I gave God permission to help get me out. A year and a half later, the other person became involved with someone else and that was my ticket to leave.

The conviction was stronger now and in January of 1986 I moved out of that house and relationship. I started reading the Bible, went to Christian Counseling and joined a prayer group and found my release. A Scripture that grabbed my heart said;

"It was for freedom that Christ set us

free; therefore keep standing firm and do not be subject again to a yoke of slavery."
Galatians 5:1

I consider lesbianism slavery because it is lived in an atmosphere of self-hatred. Then, one finds herself falling to food and alcohol addictions to cover the pain and the shame.

Spiritually, I felt disobedient to God. But I also felt in my heart His love toward me. Christian counselors helped to reveal God's love for me and complete forgiveness for this sin. Ezekiel 16:4-15 was especially helpful. [1]

I began praying for a spouse. I did meet a man and we started dating. Six weeks into the relationship I opened up to him and told him my story. His love superseded my pain and we were

---

[1] Find Ezekiel 16:4-15 on page 90

eventually married. We now have two lovely children and have been married over twenty-five years.

If I could give some advice to anyone struggling with the homosexual lifestyle, I would encourage you to do these three things:

1. Pray for God's help. He loves you and will work on your behalf.
2. Get spiritual counselling. God's Word is alive and powerful and will direct your steps.
3. Tell someone you are struggling. No one needs to fight this fight alone.

If you would like to contact me and get some help with your struggle with homosexuality, you can use the author's email found at the end of this book and he will contact me.

Thank you and God bless you,

Shelley,

A New Woman in Christ.

Chapter 15

Stand Strong

As we get ready to close our book on this very socially, controversial subject, I would like to leave you with some words of encouragement to help you to "stand strong" in this debate.

I have chosen one proverb from each chapter of the Book of Proverbs. They are sharp, concise and right to the point. May they strengthen you in your decision to remain Godly in this upside down world.

He who listens to me (wisdom) shall live
securely And will be at ease from the
dread of evil.   Pr 1:33

For the LORD gives wisdom; From His
mouth come knowledge and
understanding.   Pr 2:6

Trust in the LORD with all your heart And
do not lean on your own
understanding.   Pr 3:5

The way of the wicked is like darkness;
They do not know over what they
stumble.   Pr 4:19

Let your fountain be blessed, And rejoice
in the wife of your youth.   Pr 5:18

For the commandment is a lamp and the
teaching is light; And reproofs for
discipline are the way of life.   Pr 6:23

Keep my commandments and live, And my
teaching as the apple of your eye.

Pr 7:2

For wisdom is better than jewels; And all
desirable things cannot compare with
her. Pr 8:11

The fear of the LORD is the beginning of
wisdom, And the knowledge of the Holy
One is understanding. Pr 9:10

Riches do not profit in the day of wrath,
But righteousness delivers from death.

Pr 11:4

The way of a fool is right in his own eyes,
But a wise man is he who listens to
counsel. Pr 12:15

He who walks with wise men will be wise,
But the companion of fools will suffer
harm.   Pr 13:20

There is a way which seems right to a
man, But its end is the way of death.
                                   Pr 14:12

Righteousness exalts a nation, But sin is a
disgrace to any people.   Pr 14:34

A scoffer does not love one who reproves
him, He will not go to the wise.
                                   Pr 15:12

He who is slow to anger is better than the
mighty, And he who rules his spirit,
than he who captures a city.   Pr 16:32
He who justifies the wicked and he who
condemns the righteous, Both of them
alike are an abomination to the LORD.
                                   Pr 17:15

To show partiality to the wicked is not
    good, Nor to thrust aside the righteous
    in judgment.   Pr 18:5

He who keeps the commandment keeps
    his soul, But he who is careless of
    conduct will die.   Pr 19:16

A righteous man who walks in his
    integrity-- How blessed are his sons
    after him.   Pr 20:7

There is no wisdom and no understanding
    And no counsel against the LORD.
        Pr 21:30

Do not move the ancient boundary Which
    your fathers have set.   Pr 22:28

Do not let your heart envy sinners, But
    live in the fear of the LORD always.
        Pr 23:17

If you say, "See, we did not know this,"
Does He not consider it who weighs the
hearts? And does He not know it who
keeps your soul? And will He not
render to man according to his work?
Pr 24:12

Like a trampled spring and a polluted well
Is a righteous man who gives way
before the wicked.   Pr 25:26

Do not answer a fool according to his folly,
Or you will also be like him.   Pr 26:4

Be wise, my son, and make my heart glad,
That I may reply to him who
reproaches me.   Pr 27:11

Because of the sin of the land, its troubles
are increased; but by a man of wisdom
and knowledge they will be put out like
a fire.   (Bible In Basic English) Pr 28:2

When the righteous increase, the people
    rejoice, But when a wicked man rules,
    people groan.   Pr 29:2

Without guidance from God law and order
    disappear, but God blesses everyone
    who obeys his Law. (Contemporary
    English Version)   v. 18

There is a kind who is pure in his own
    eyes, Yet is not washed from his
    filthiness.   Pr 30:12

Open your mouth, judge righteously, And
    defend the rights of the afflicted and
    needy.   Pr 31:9

Summary

Homosexuality is a condition which is an attraction to the same sex. God does not judge us based on our conditions. Homosexuality is judged when it becomes a behavior. We are all responsible for our behaviors.

The cause is not genetic, it is spiritual. The tendency or inclination cannot be helped but the behavior can be controlled.

The Bible is clear that the practice of homosexuality keeps people out of the kingdom of God. God loves the homosexual but He cannot bring a person that is not regenerated by the Holy Spirit into heaven.

The attitude of Christians toward the homosexual should always be one of love and respect. God loved us before we responded to His offer of salvation so we should do the same for others.

God demonstrates His own love toward us, in that while we were yet sinners, Christ died for us.
Romans 5:8

He didn't die for those who got it right. He died for everyone when no one got it right.

Whether you are a homosexual or not, do the best you can to live your life for God. This does not diminish God's joy for you. You can live a full life in service to Him and find more joy and contentment doing that than in any other way. God has a plan for everyone. So everyone has an opportunity to find purpose and fulfillment in Him.

ENDNOTES

Ezekiel 16:4-15

As for your birth, on the day you were
born your navel cord was not cut, nor
were you washed with water for
cleansing; you were not rubbed with
salt or even wrapped in cloths.

"No eye looked with pity on you to do any
of these things for you, to have
compassion on you. Rather you were
thrown out into the open field, for you
were abhorred on the day you were
born.

"When I passed by you and saw you
squirming in your blood, I said to you
while you were in your blood, 'Live!'
Yes, I said to you *while you were* in
your blood, 'Live!'

"I made you numerous like plants of the
field. Then you grew up, became tall

and reached the age for fine
ornaments; *your* breasts were formed
and your hair had grown. Yet you were
naked and bare.

"Then I passed by you and saw you, and
behold, you were at the time for love; so
I spread My skirt over you and covered
your nakedness. I also swore to you
and entered into a covenant with you
so that you became Mine," declares the
Lord GOD.

"Then I bathed you with water, washed off
your blood from you and anointed you
with oil.

"I also clothed you with embroidered cloth
and put sandals of porpoise skin on
your feet; and I wrapped you with fine
linen and covered you with silk.

"I adorned you with ornaments, put
bracelets on your hands and a necklace
around your neck.

"I also put a ring in your nostril, earrings
in your ears and a beautiful crown on
your head.

"Thus you were adorned with gold and
silver, and your dress was of fine linen,
silk and embroidered cloth. You ate
fine flour, honey and oil; so you were
exceedingly beautiful and advanced to
royalty.

"Then your fame went forth among the
nations on account of your beauty, for
it was perfect because of My splendor
which I bestowed on you," declares the
Lord GOD.

"But you trusted in your beauty and
played the harlot because of your fame,
and you poured out your harlotries on
every passer-by who might be *willing.*

ABOUT THE AUTHOR

David P. Therrien

Graduated from Gordon Conwell Seminary in Boston, MA with a Masters of Arts Degree In Urban Ministry. He enjoys the four seasons of New England with his wife, Donna and has three sons, Michael, David Jr. and Alex.

Dave writes on matters of faith and encouragement and pastors the wonderful people of New Hope Christian Church in Swansea, MA.

www.newhopecc.tv

MEDIA
Check out Dave's radio show
WARV 1590 am dial
Or
Stream it at
WARV.net
Weekdays at 12:30 pm E.T. and
Saturdays at 3 pm.

DVDs & CDs can also be found at
www.newhopecc.tv
MEDIA button

DAVE'S BLOG
www.think2wice.co

POCKETBOOK SERIES
So far...
Look Up And Be Forgiven VOL.1
Going Forward In Faith VOL.2
How To Escape From Guilt & Shame VOL.3
Grace, Kindness & Righteousness VOL. 4
The Loving Father & The Lost Son VOL. 5
The Brightest Future Ever VOL. 6
My Spiritual Journey VOL. 7
A Christmas Reflection VOL. 8
Questions About Salvation VOL. 9
Proverbs For Men VOL. 10
Proverbs For Women VOL. 11

Other books
Beauty In Darkness
Finding HOPE In Distressing Times
GOT Life?
How To Know If You're Really Living
Angel Conversations
Sailing Through Storms
Recovering Lost Ground
*A 12 Step Guide to Overcoming Compulsive
Behaviors*
Leaving A Godly Legacy
*How You Will Be Remembered After You
Are Gone*
Bible Men Study Guide
With DVD
Questions About Salvation
Homosexuality
Good Choice or Bad Choice?
Think Twice
About What You're Going To Say Or Do
40 Day Reading Guide

Other Resources
You can find other books by
David P. Therrien
at
www.inspiringbooks.org
Email
Inspiringbooksofhope@gmail.com

For CDs and DVDs go to
www.newhopecc.tv

Life is a journey,
Don't look back and keep
moving.

23907515R00060

Made in the USA
Middletown, DE
07 September 2015